Lily's Flight
for Peace and the
Fussyoderpus

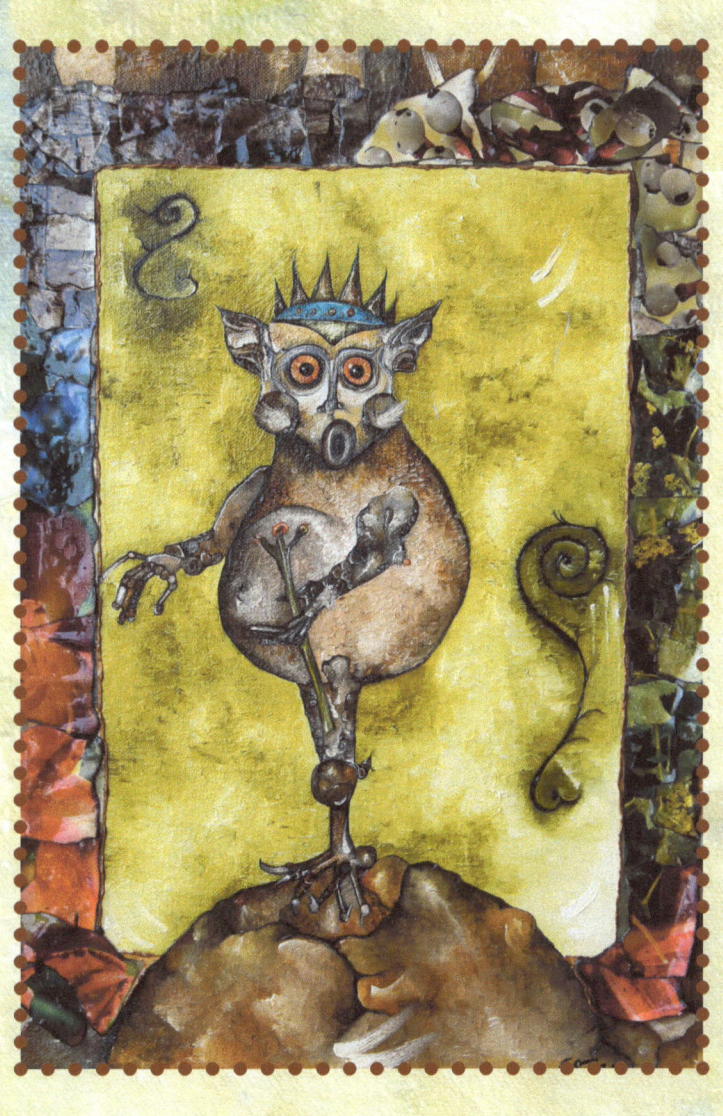

By
L E O N A   T O B I N

To order additional copies of this book, contact:
Xlibris Corporation
1-888-795-4274
www.Xlibris.com
Orders@Xlibris.com

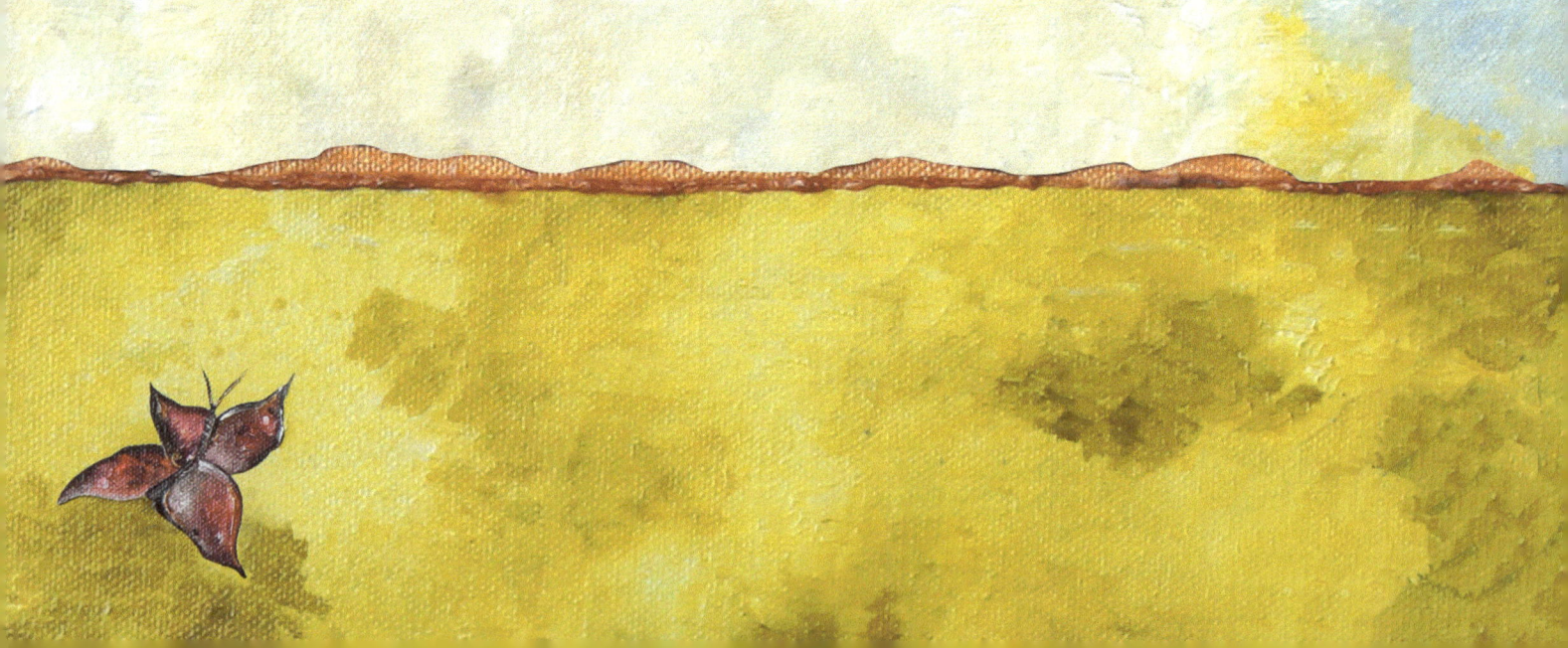

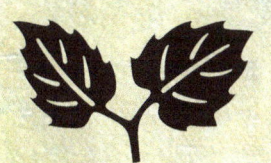

Dedicated to my darling daughters...
I love you girls dearly and I encourage you,
to challenge your mind and to follow your heart.

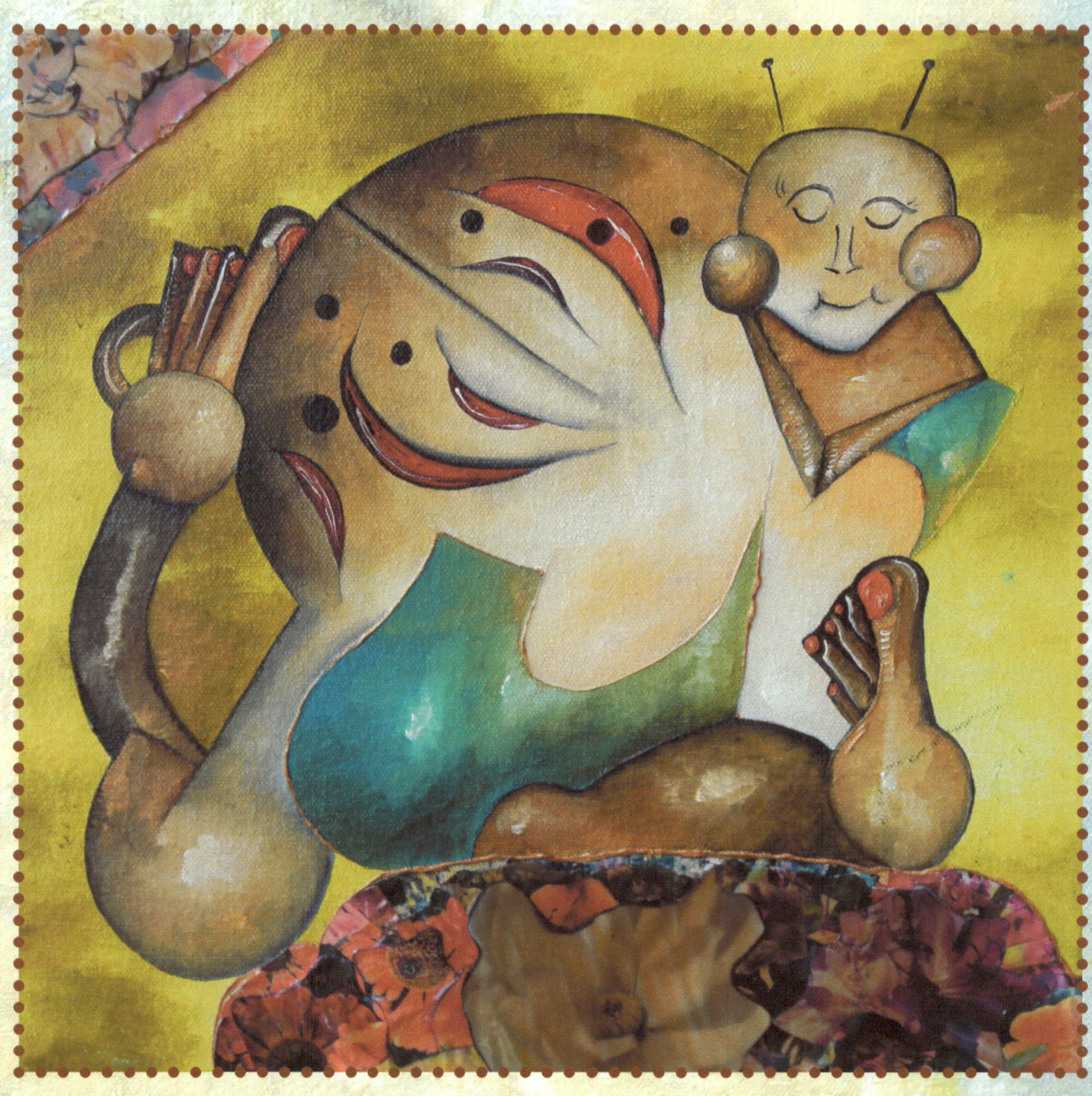

Lily, the lady bug, had a magical gleam. She loved to do things...
especially dream.

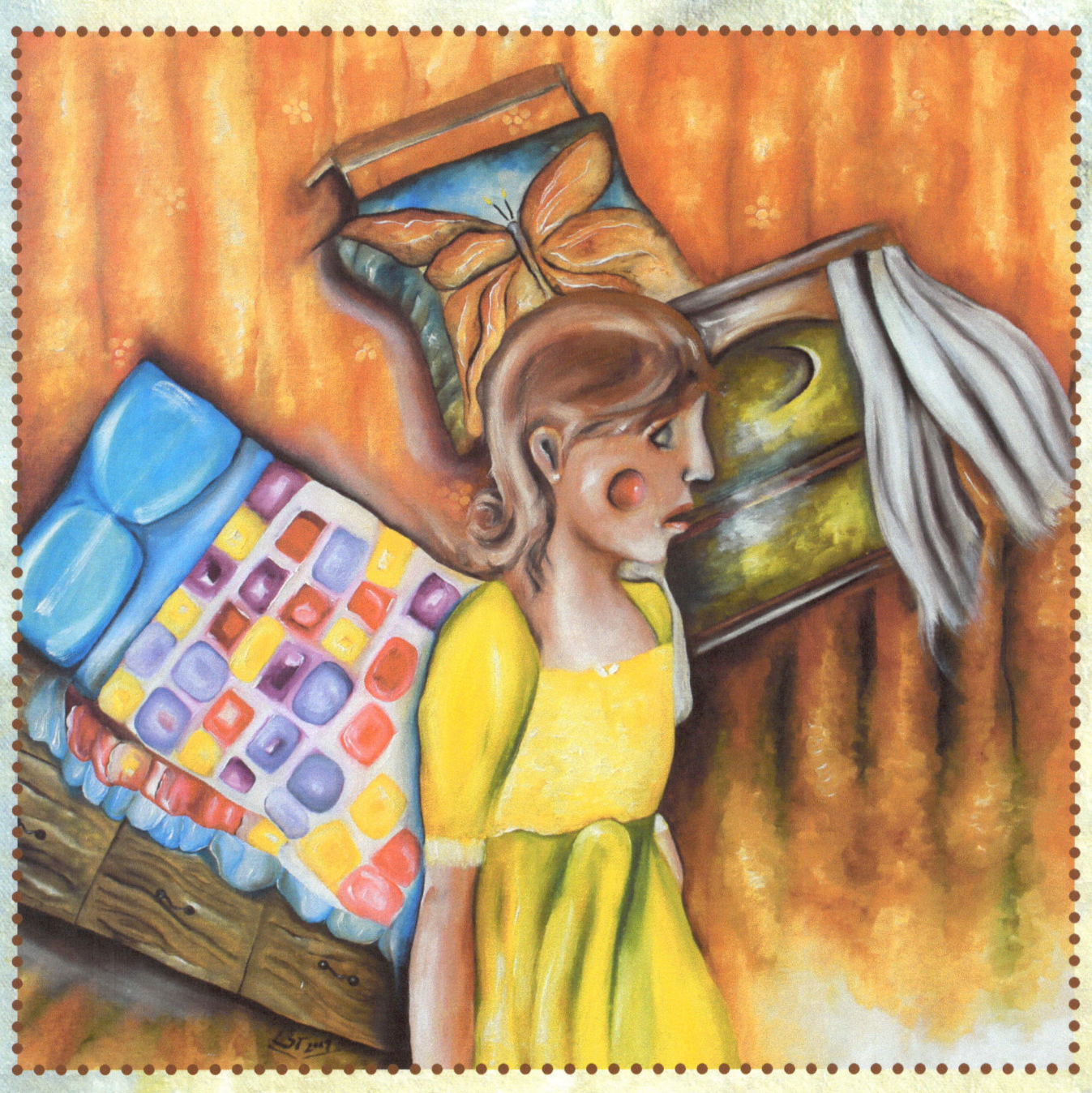

For when the moon was out, dreams would never wane. Reality
and dreams became much the same.

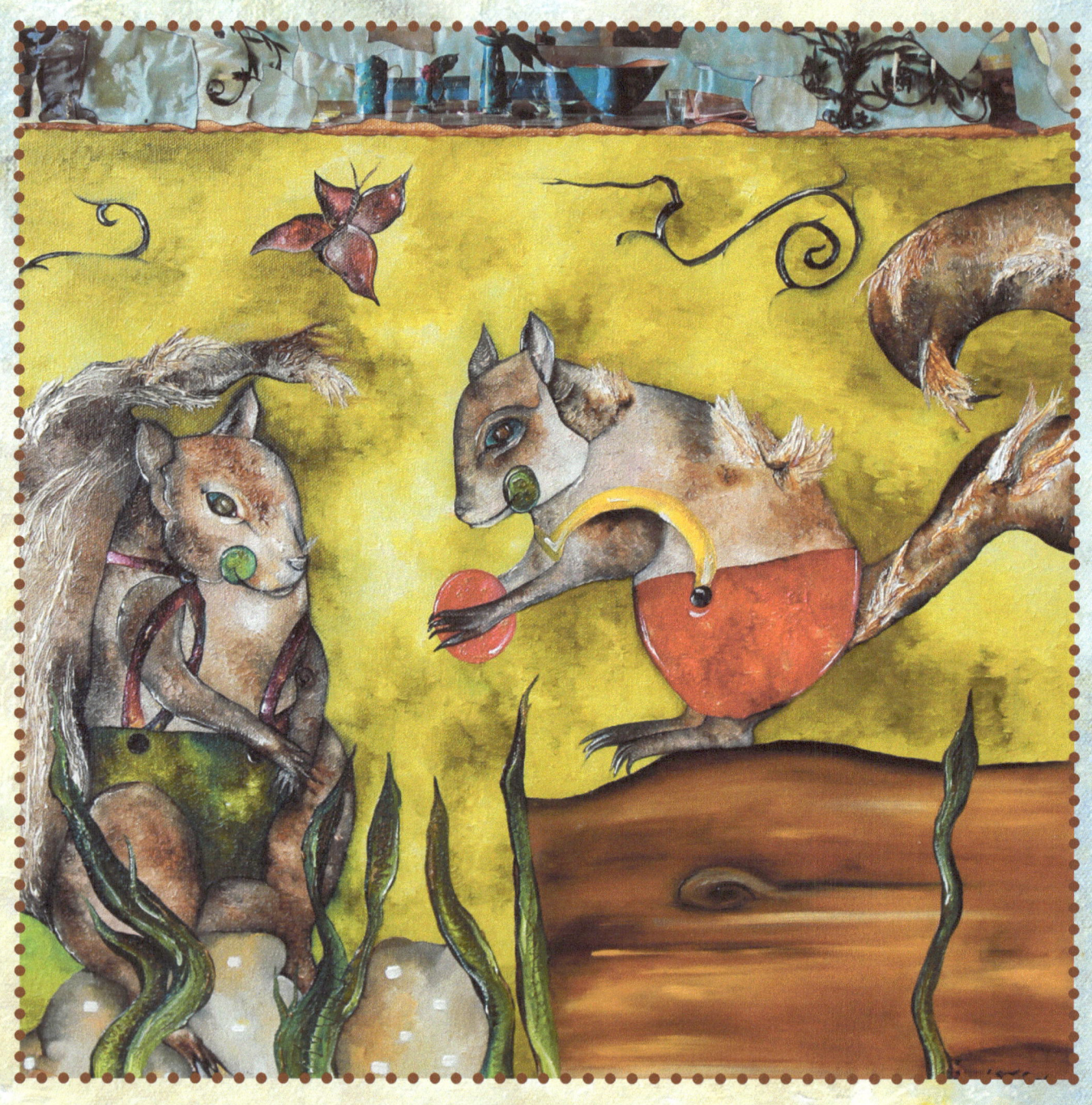

On a resting limb, Lily sat one day, listening to the squirrels
giggle and play.

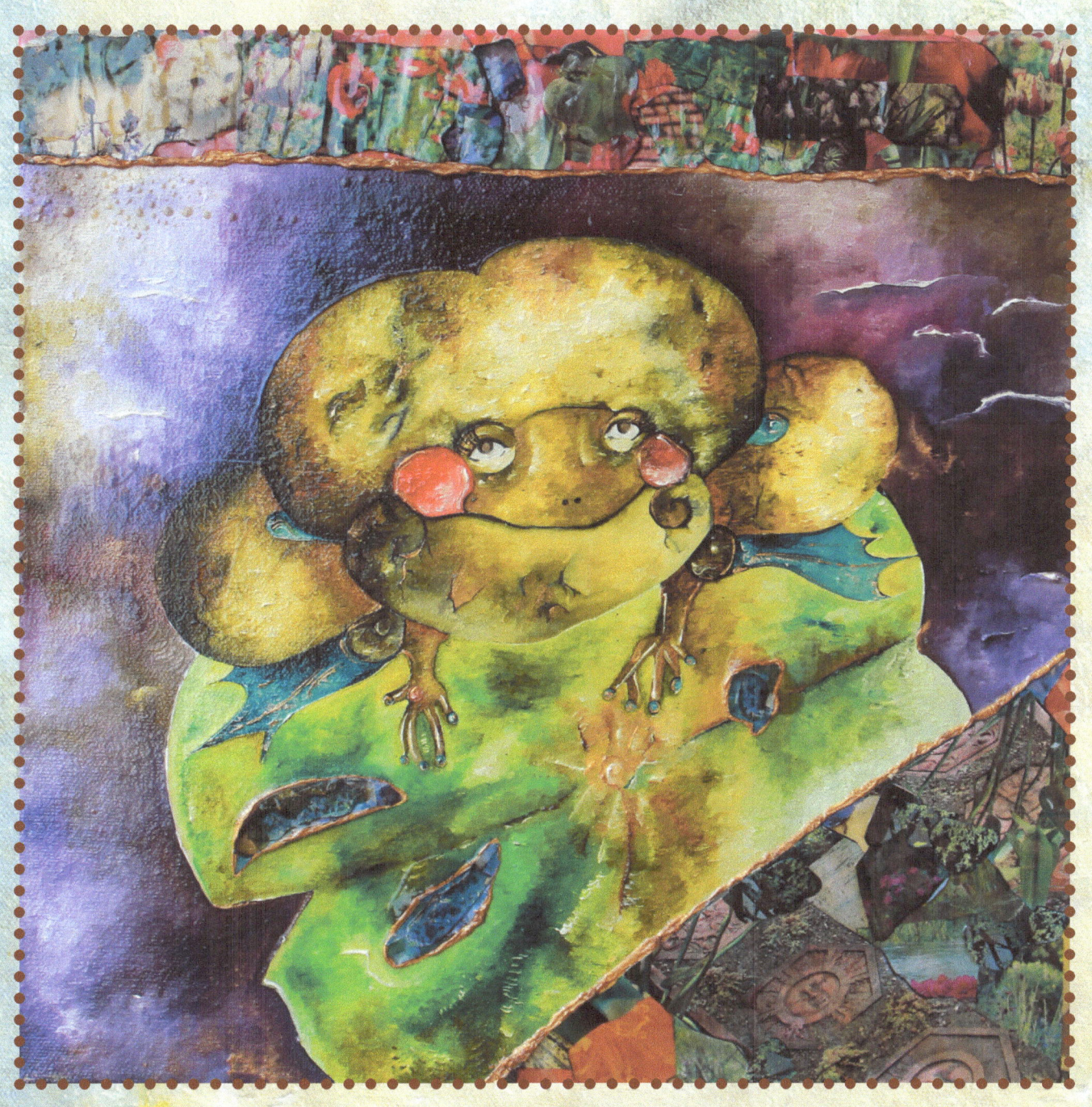

While she sat, a frog kissed her cheek. This frog's home was in a lavender creek.

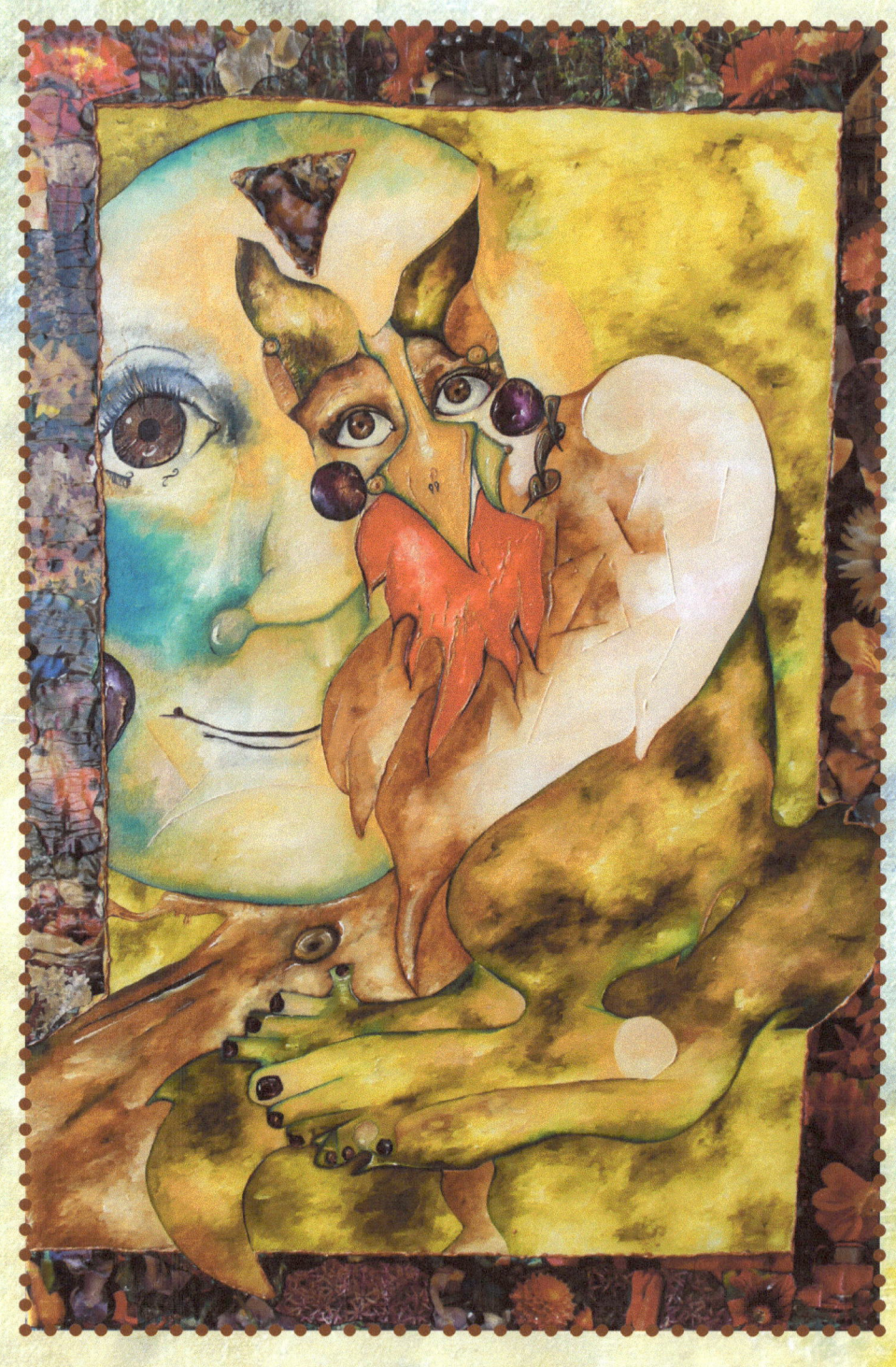

A beautiful wolfbird howled to her a tune, as she began to see the face of the moon.

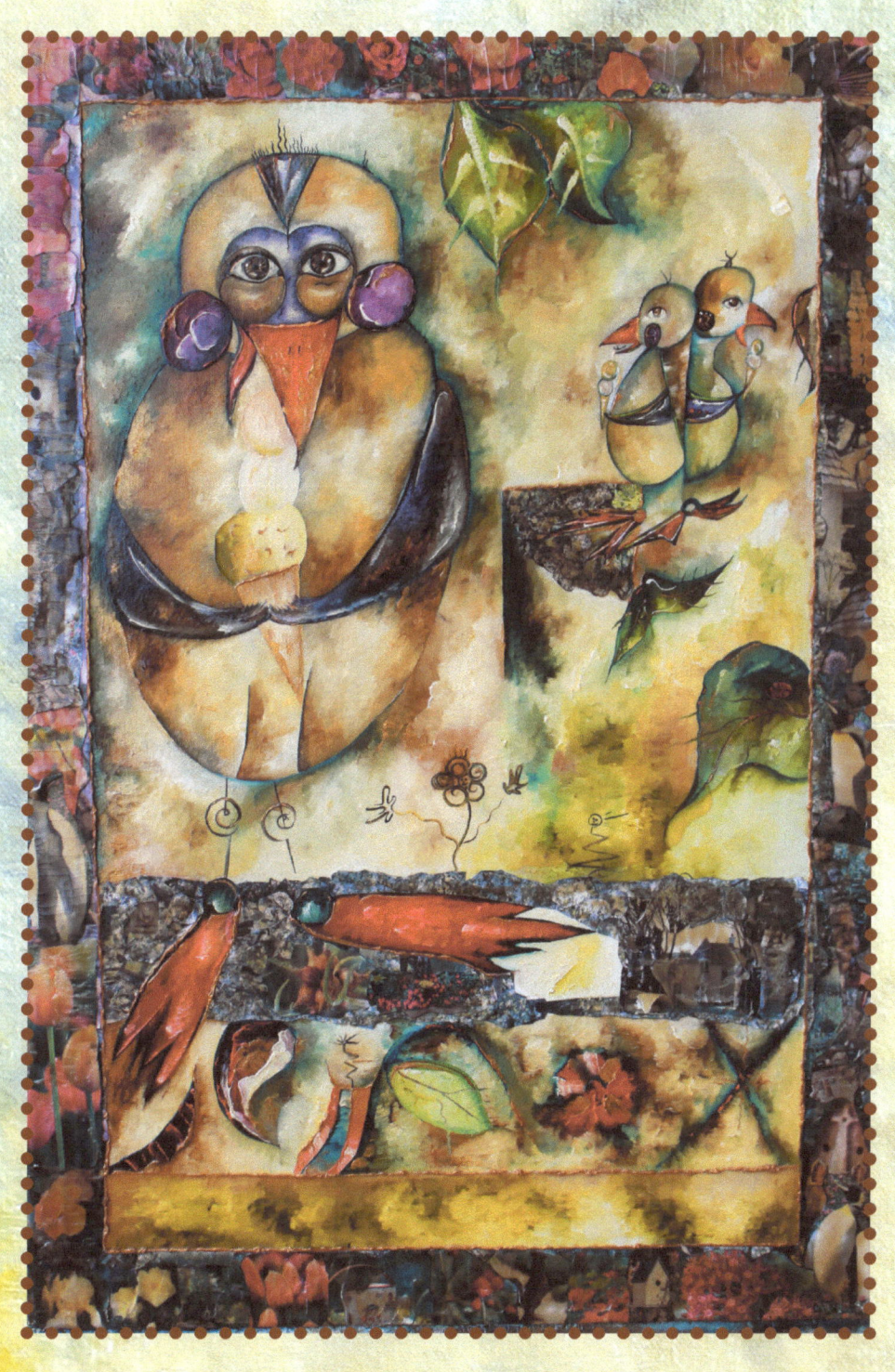

As she dozed off she began to smile. She then closed her eyes to
rest for a while. While she was resting, she began to dream,
of little penguins eating ice cream.

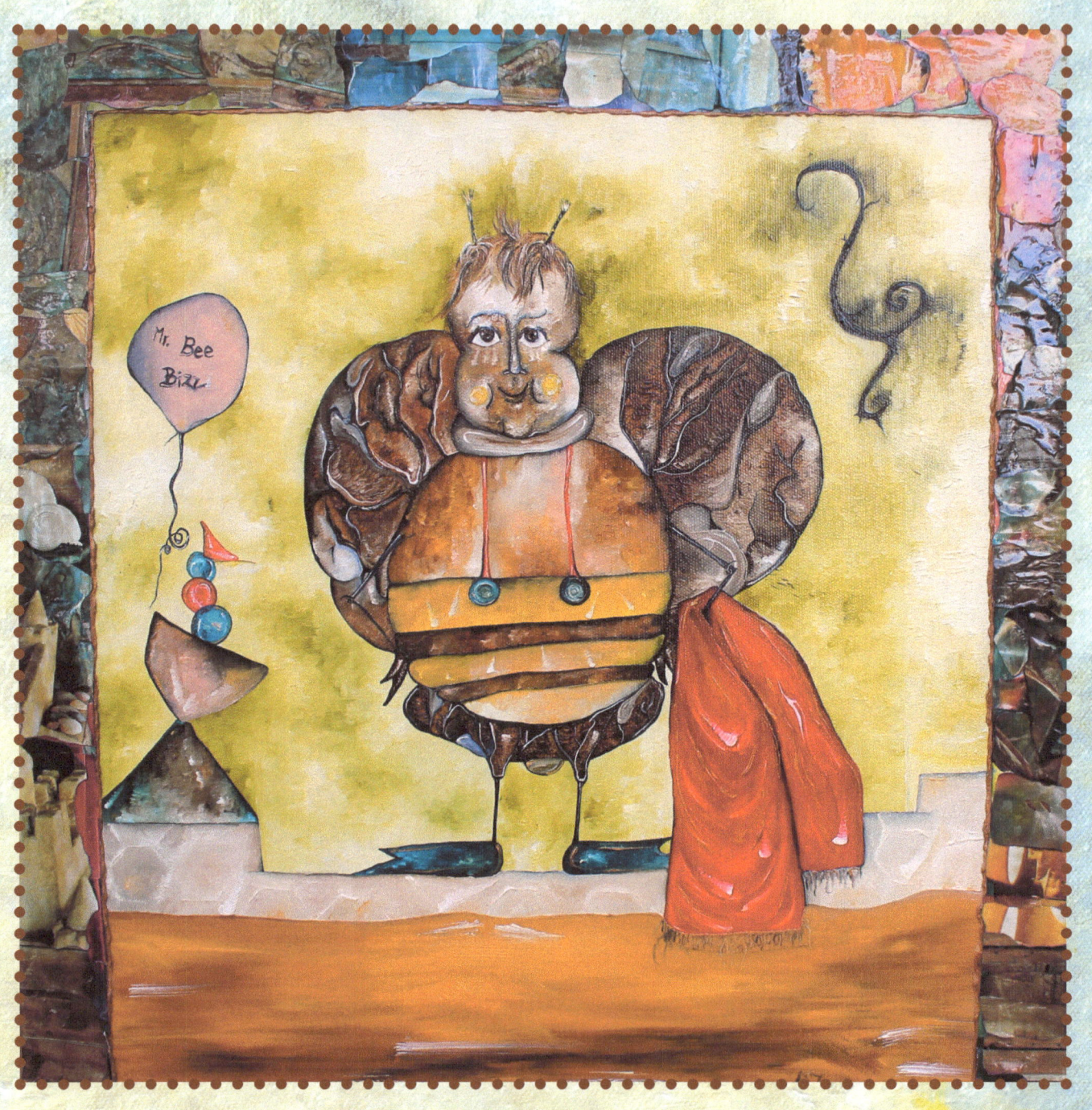

In her dream her friends acted funny. They would visit Mr. Bee Bizz and swim in his honey.

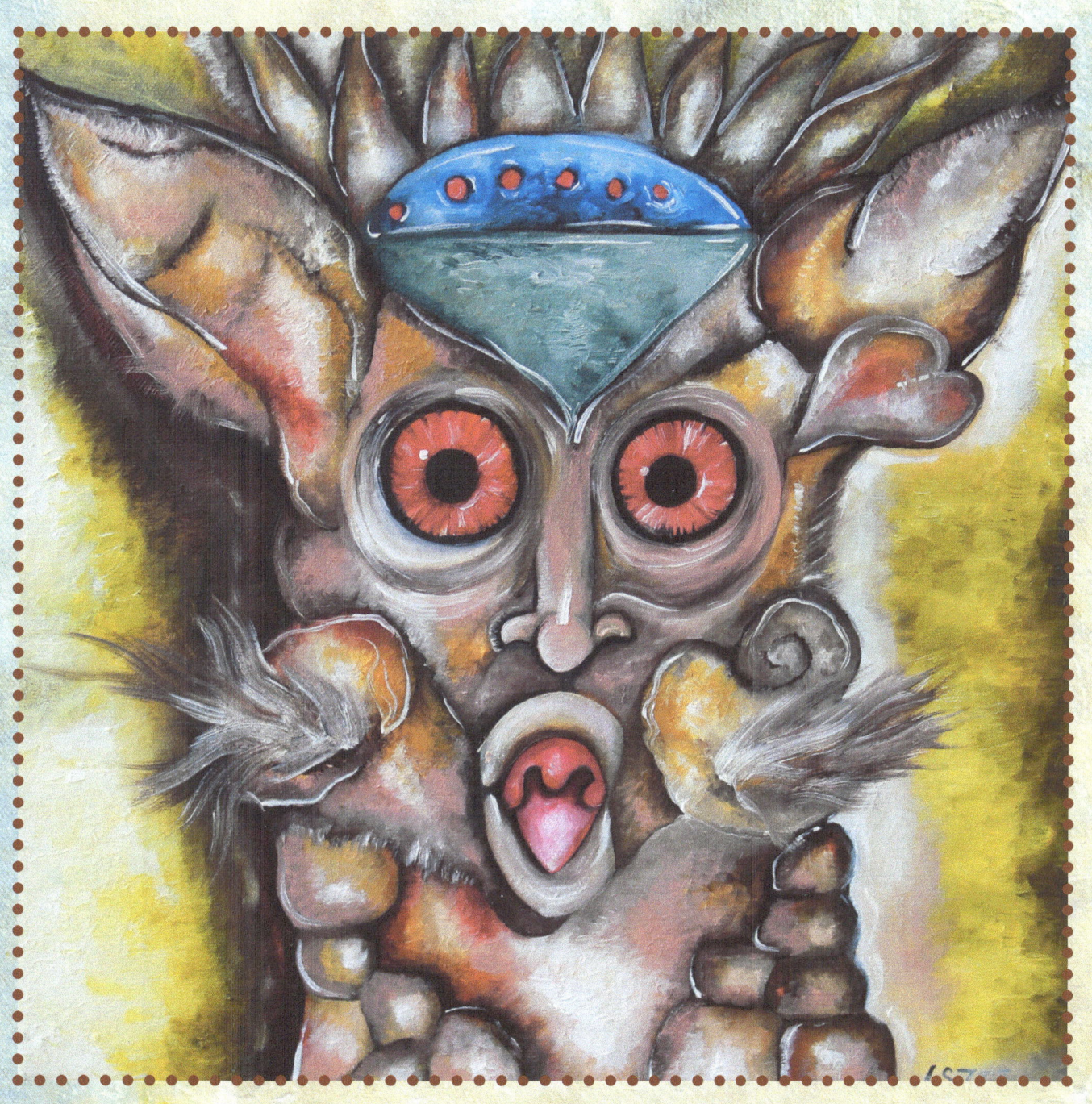

While Lily dreamed, no one was mean, except the fussyoderpus
who loved to scream.

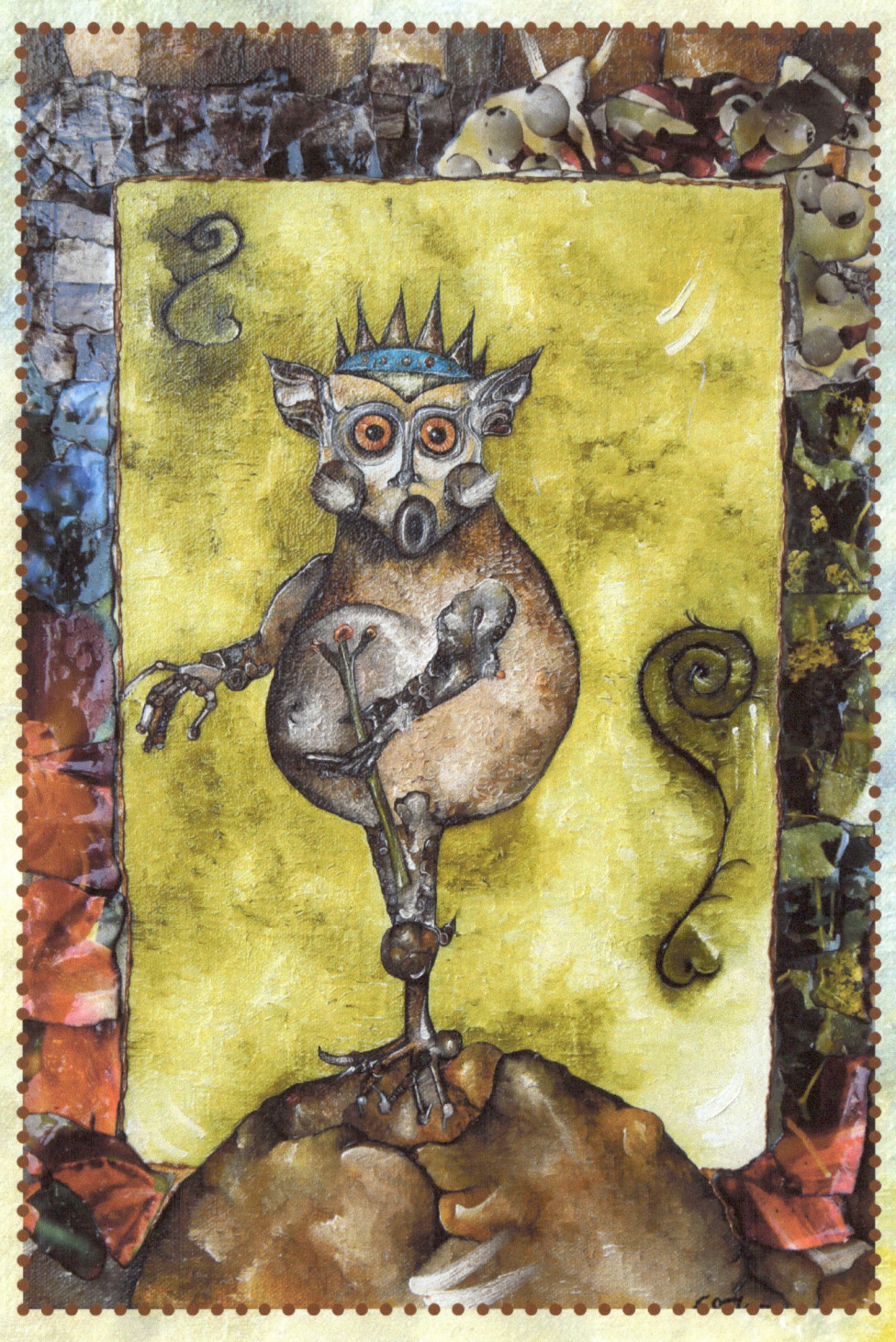

Upon his stone he stood as king. He would pick up his wand and begin to scream. He screamed in the night, as to awake all, until the day he had a fall.

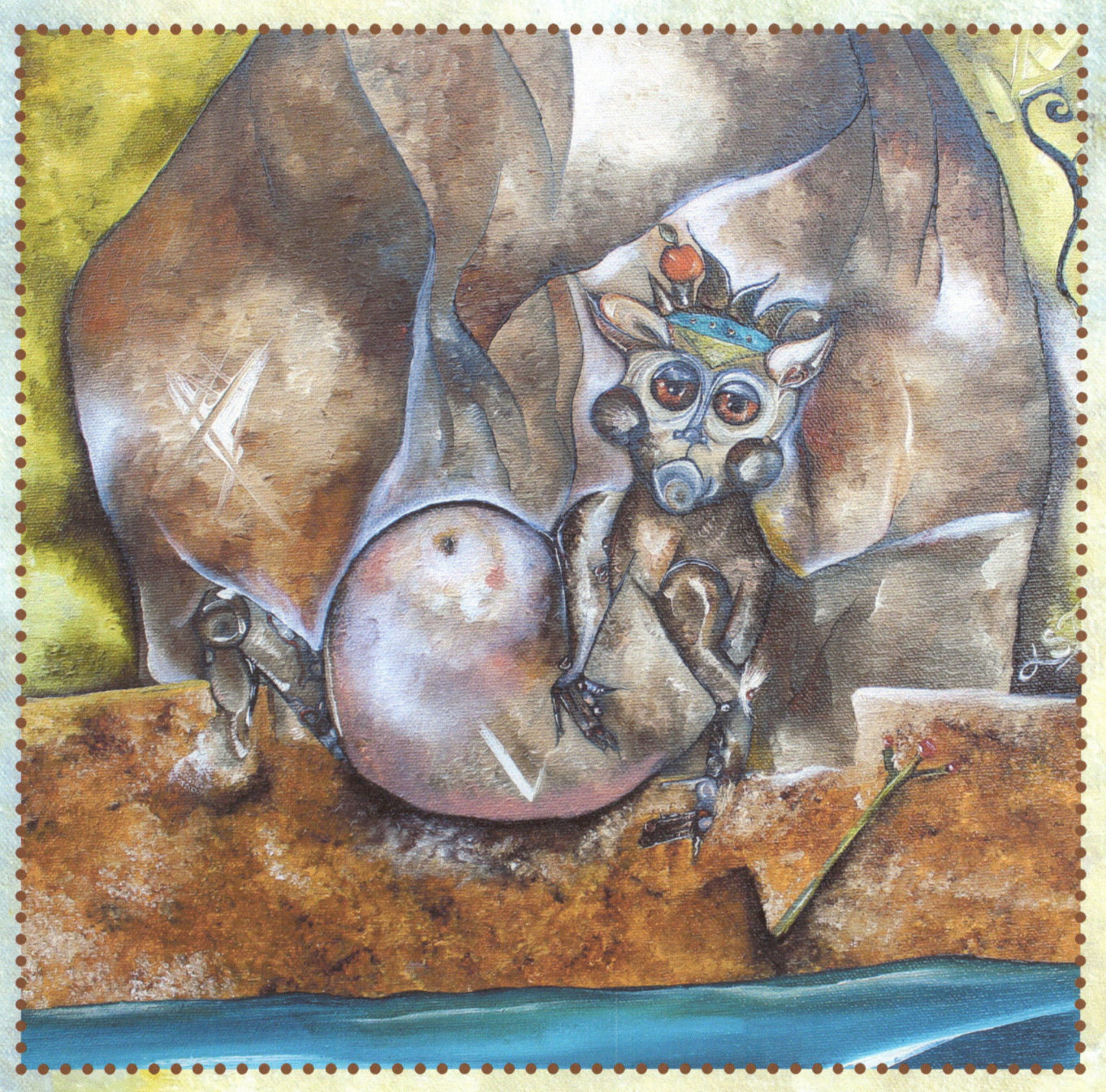

He fell from a stone that cracked when he screamed. Then he became humbled and weak, or so it seemed.

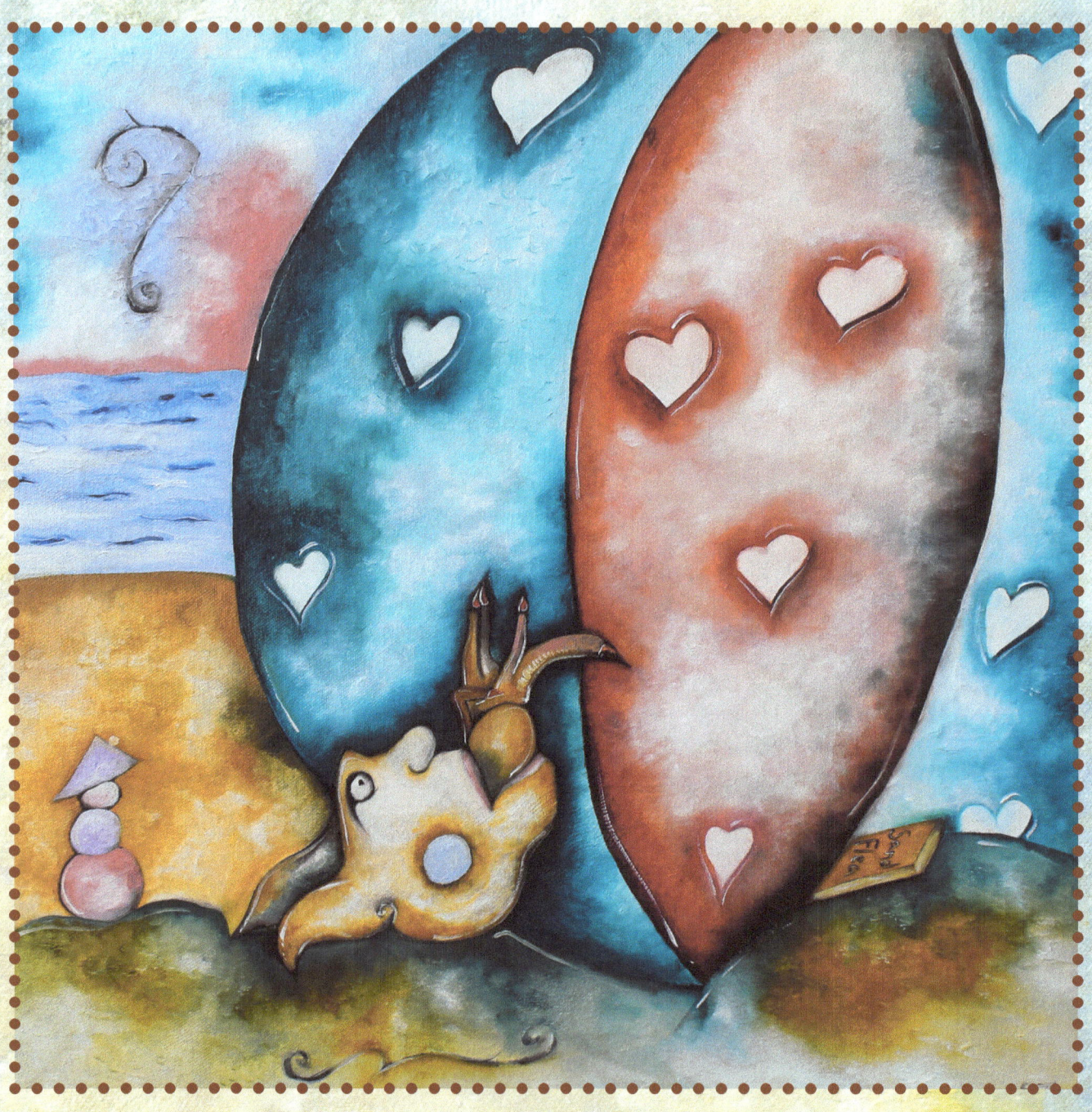

Painfully, he worried, for his foot had been lost. Had it been
hiding in the sand or had it simply run off?

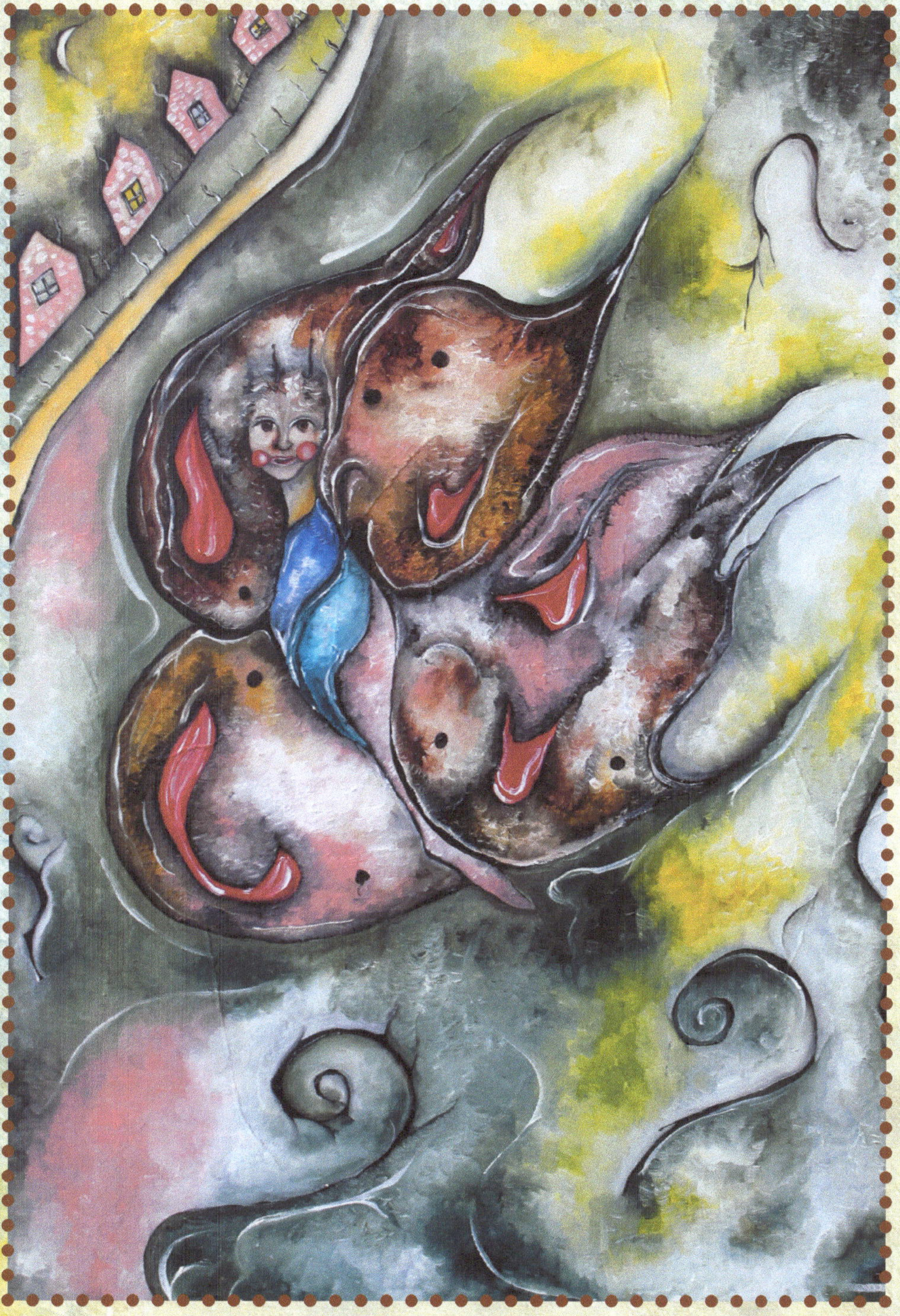

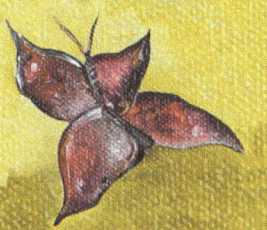

When Lily heard the Fussyoderpus cry,
she immediately began to fly.

15

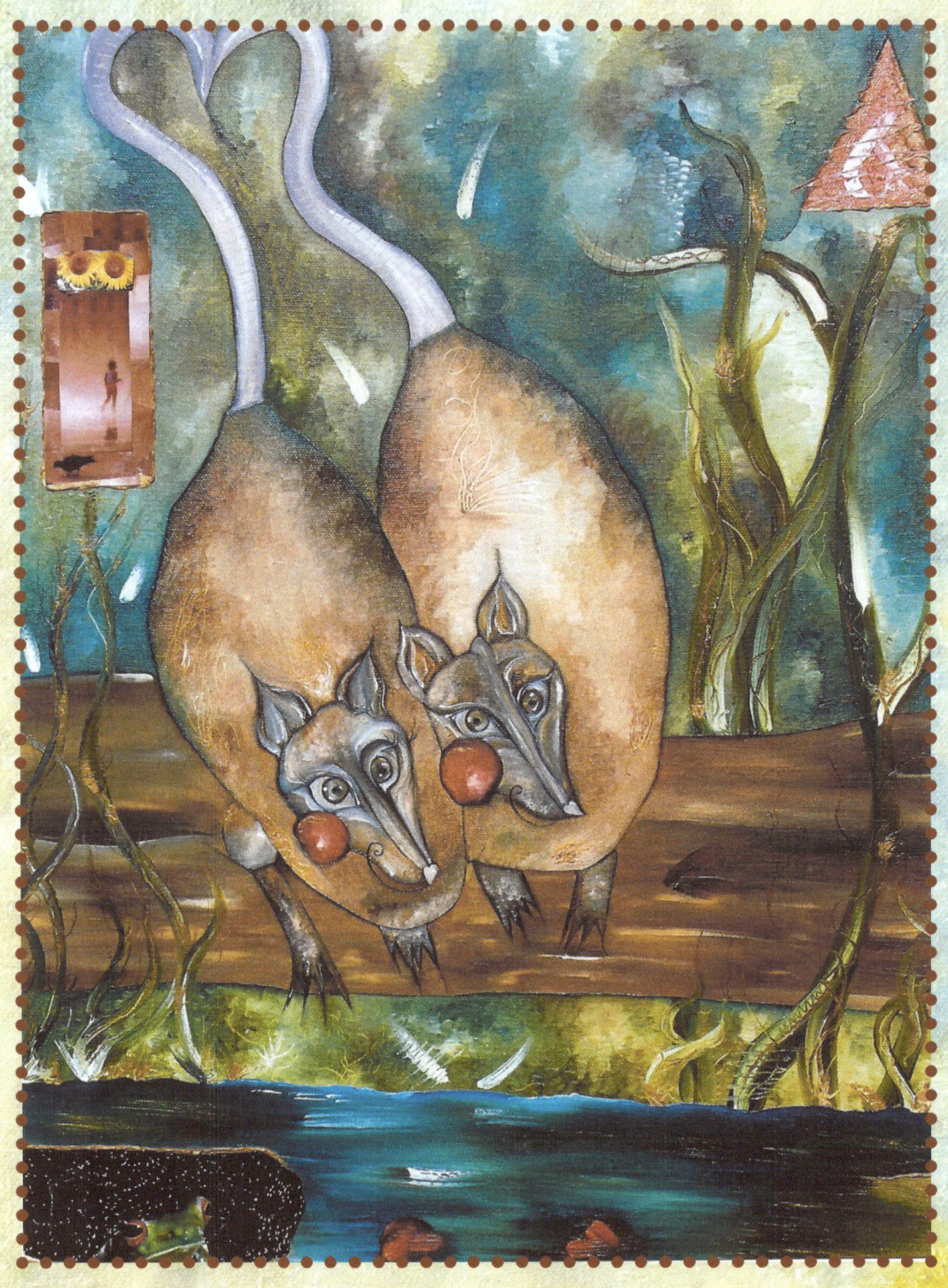

She flew past a couple of possums in love, gazing out into the
world, and at the moon up above.

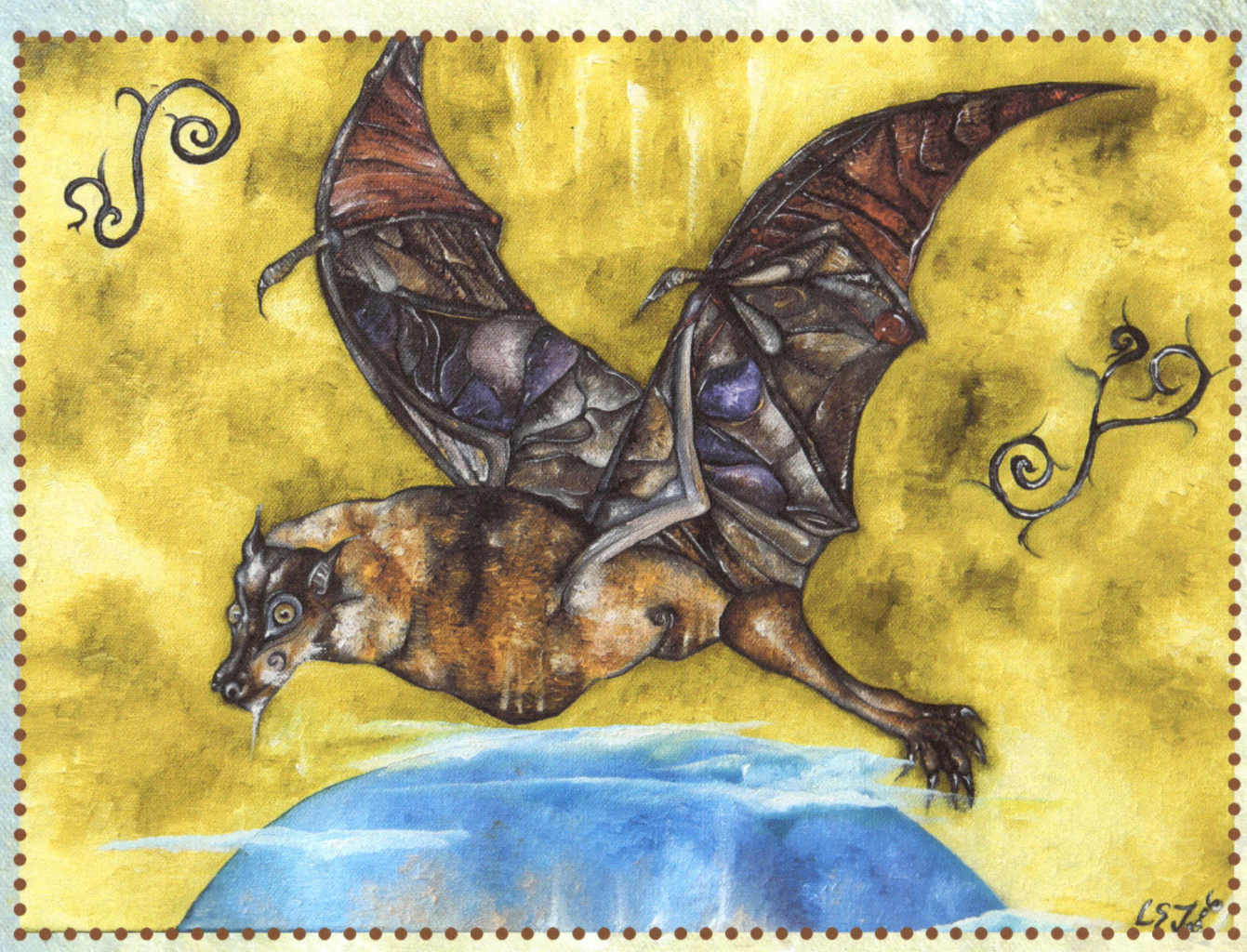

A clumsy old bat bumped his head on her wing and said, "sorry,
I'm old and I can't see a thing." Lily said, "well that's all right,"
then she continued her flight. She searched for peace and
the Fussyoderpus until she lost sight of the moon.

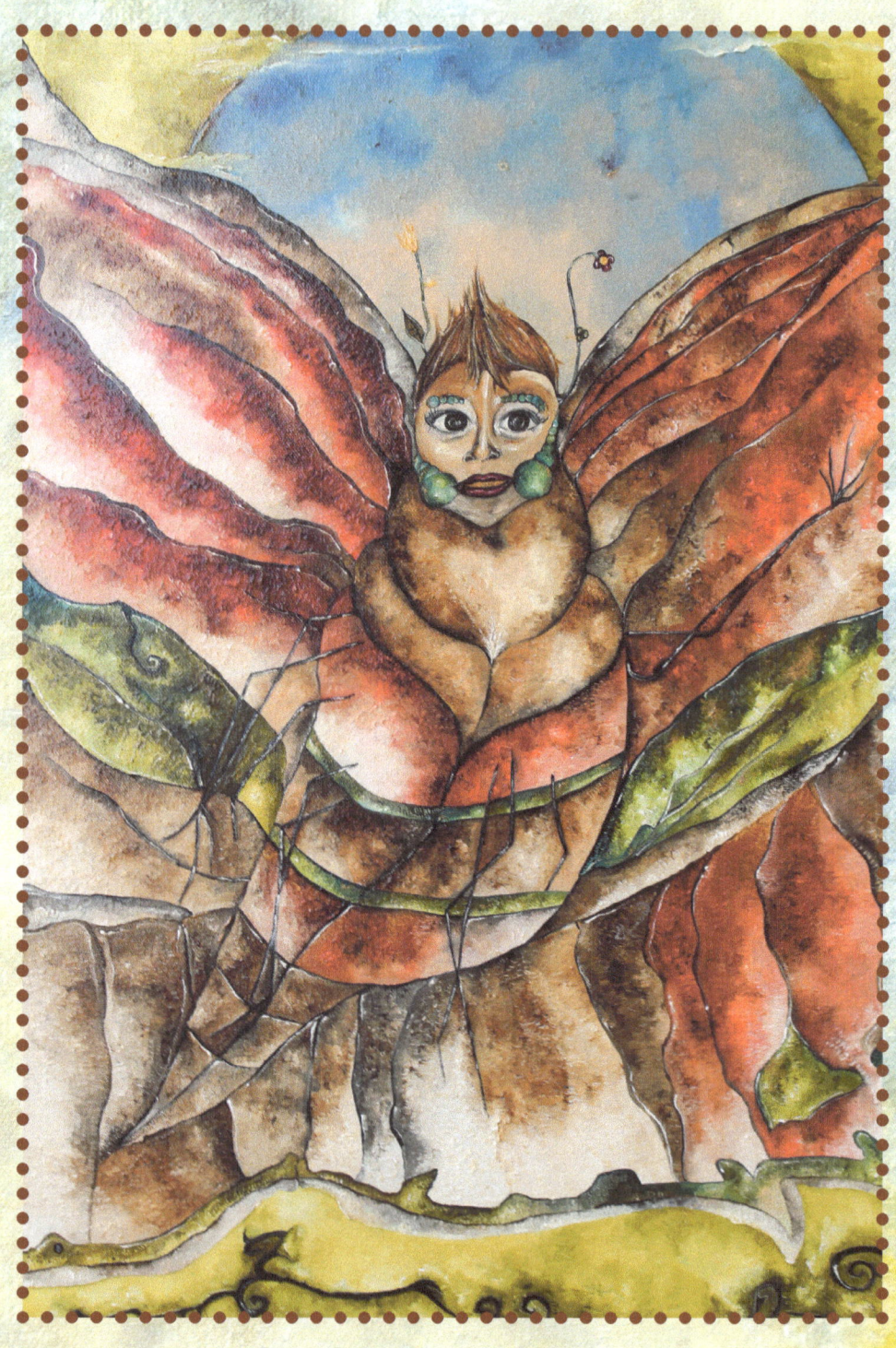

Lily was cold and afraid and became quite scared, when suddenly
Linea the butterfly appeared. Her smile could melt most any
storm, her wings were like sailing boats and she had smiling
charm. Lily and Linea held hands through the sky.
When Lily was secure, Linea waved good-bye.

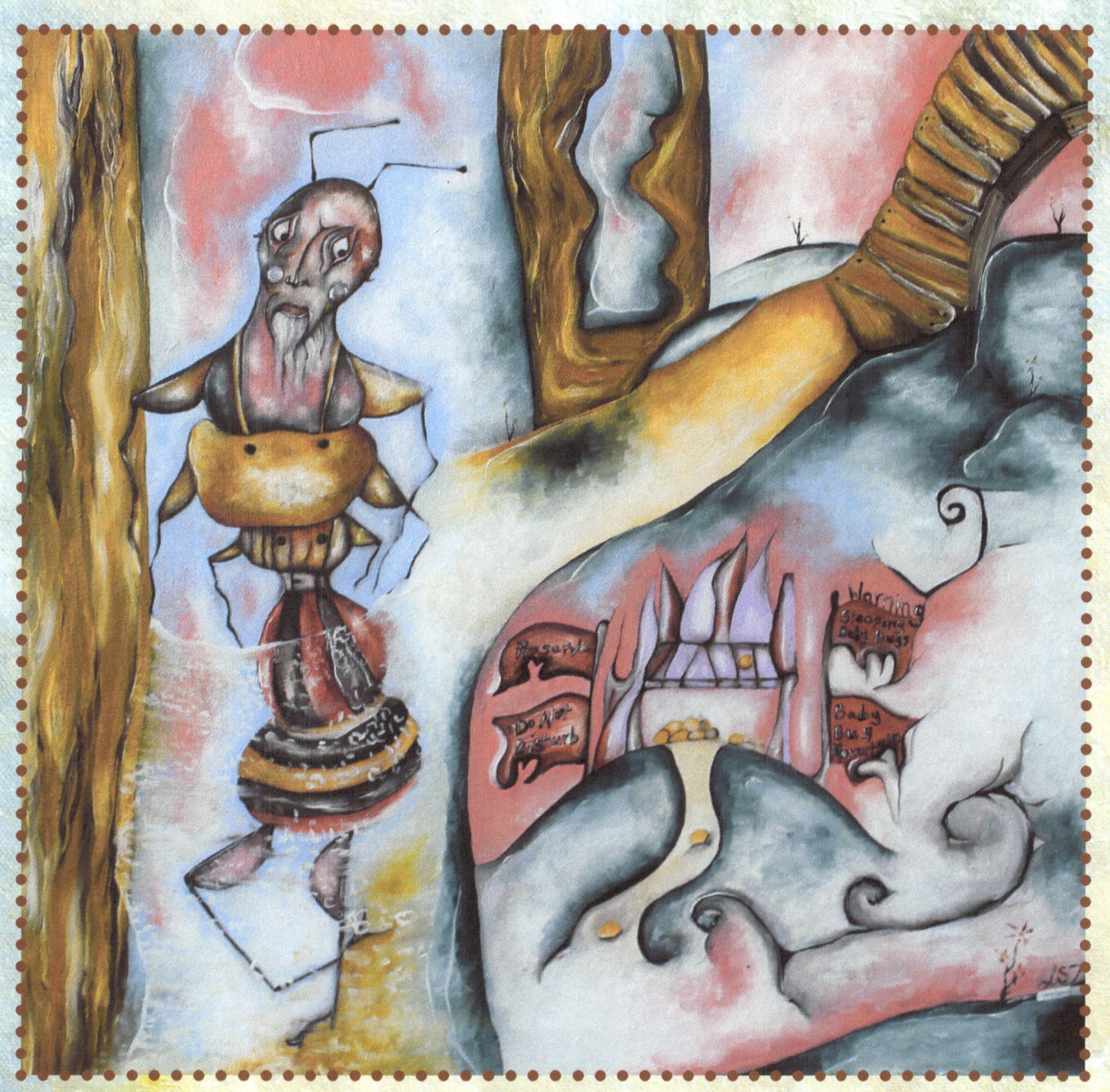

With heavy wings and a sparkling heart, Lily flew on and on until she spotted the Fussyoderpus. She rescued him from a serious ant, which had walked over a ramp and through a tree to capture the Fussyoderpus weak on one knee.

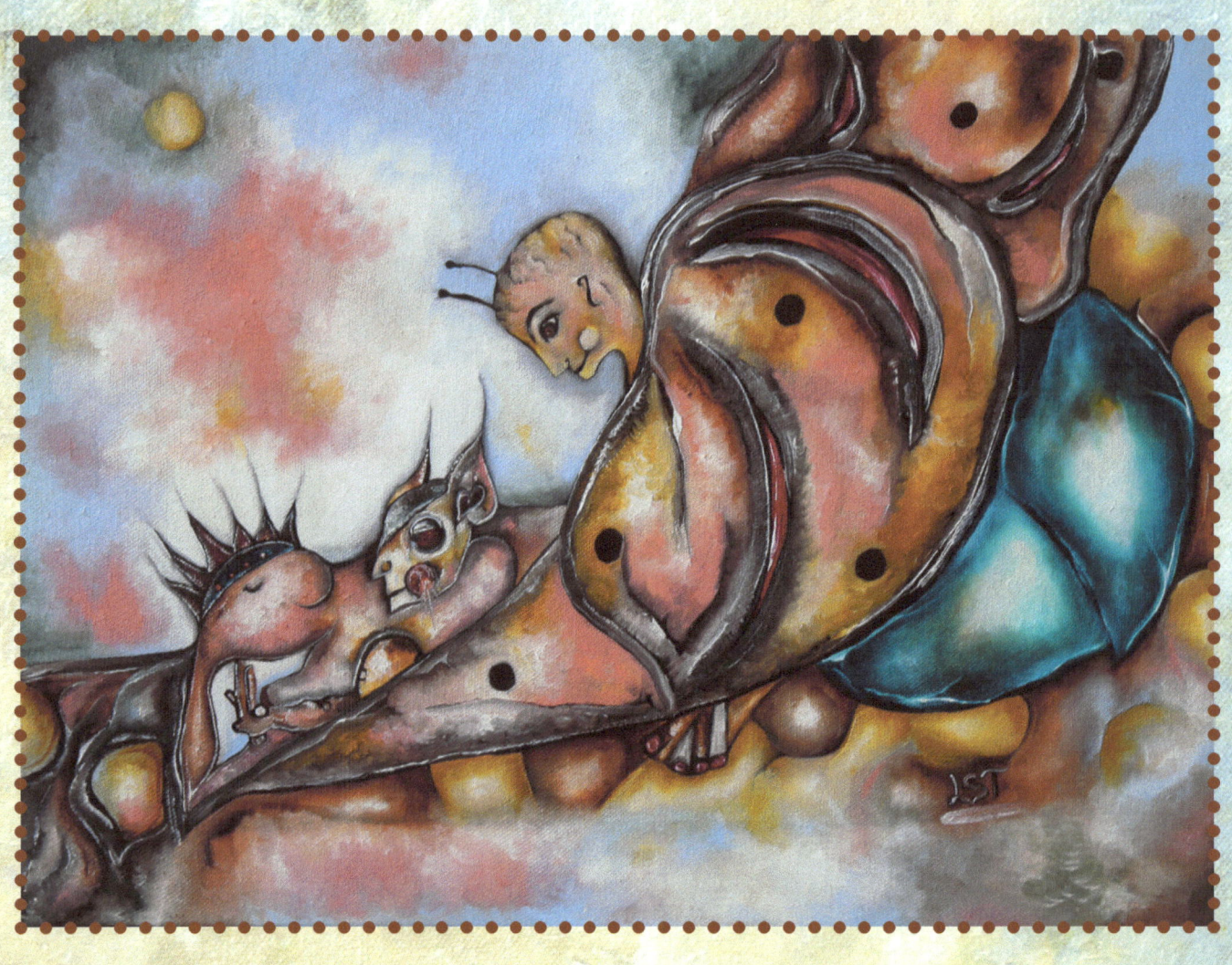

Lily lifted the Fusssyoderpus onto her wing, and he promised her that he would never again scream.

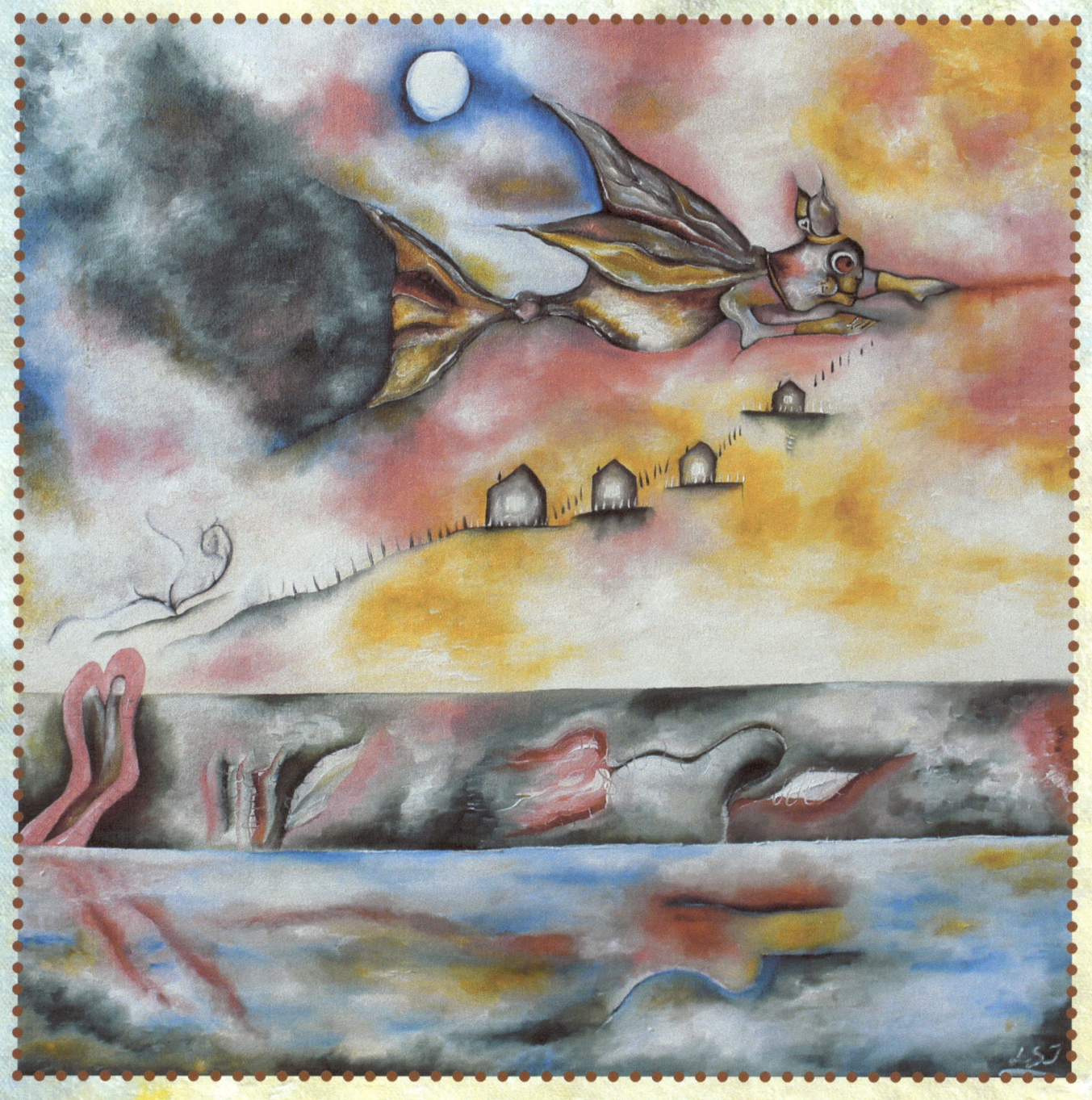

Lily was gentle in teaching the Fussyoderpus how to fly, so he practiced handstands and somersaults high in the sky.

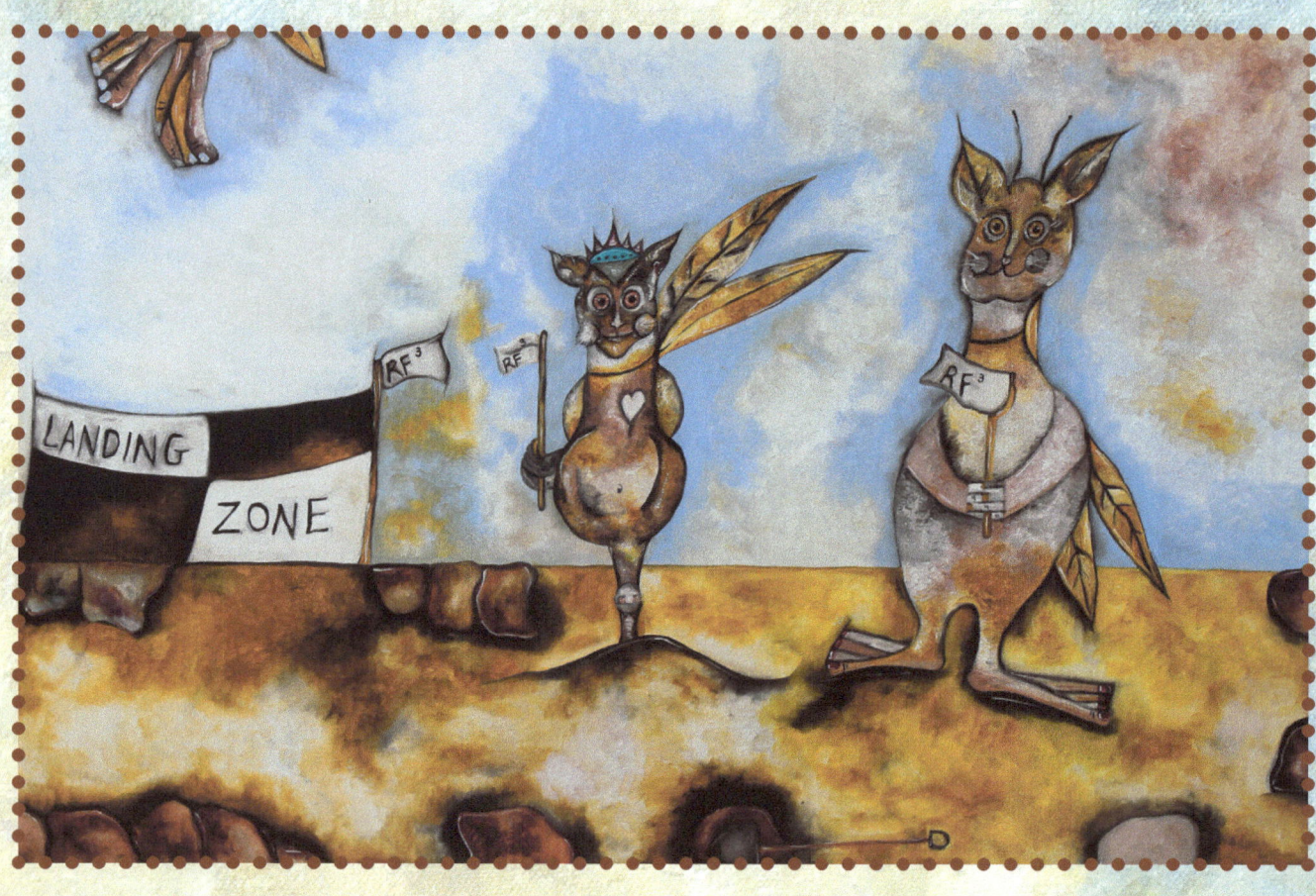

At last, the Fussyoderpus felt that his heart was true and he flew
on to join the Olympic team called Rui Flew Flew Flew. He then
went on to win prize after prize and became the
only footless Rui so small in size.

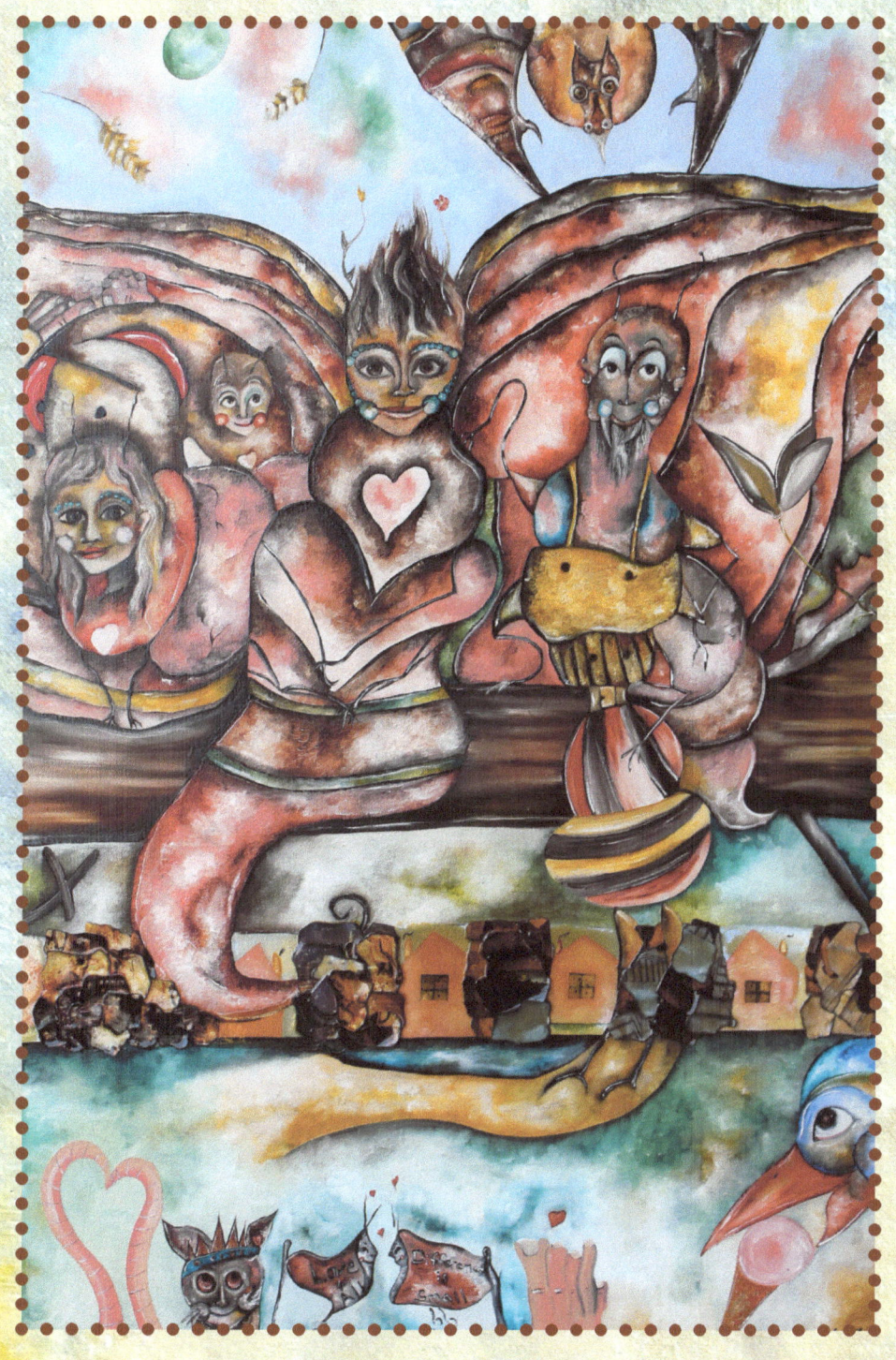

Now, dreams can dance on, once there's peace in the night. When friends help their neighbors all becomes alright.

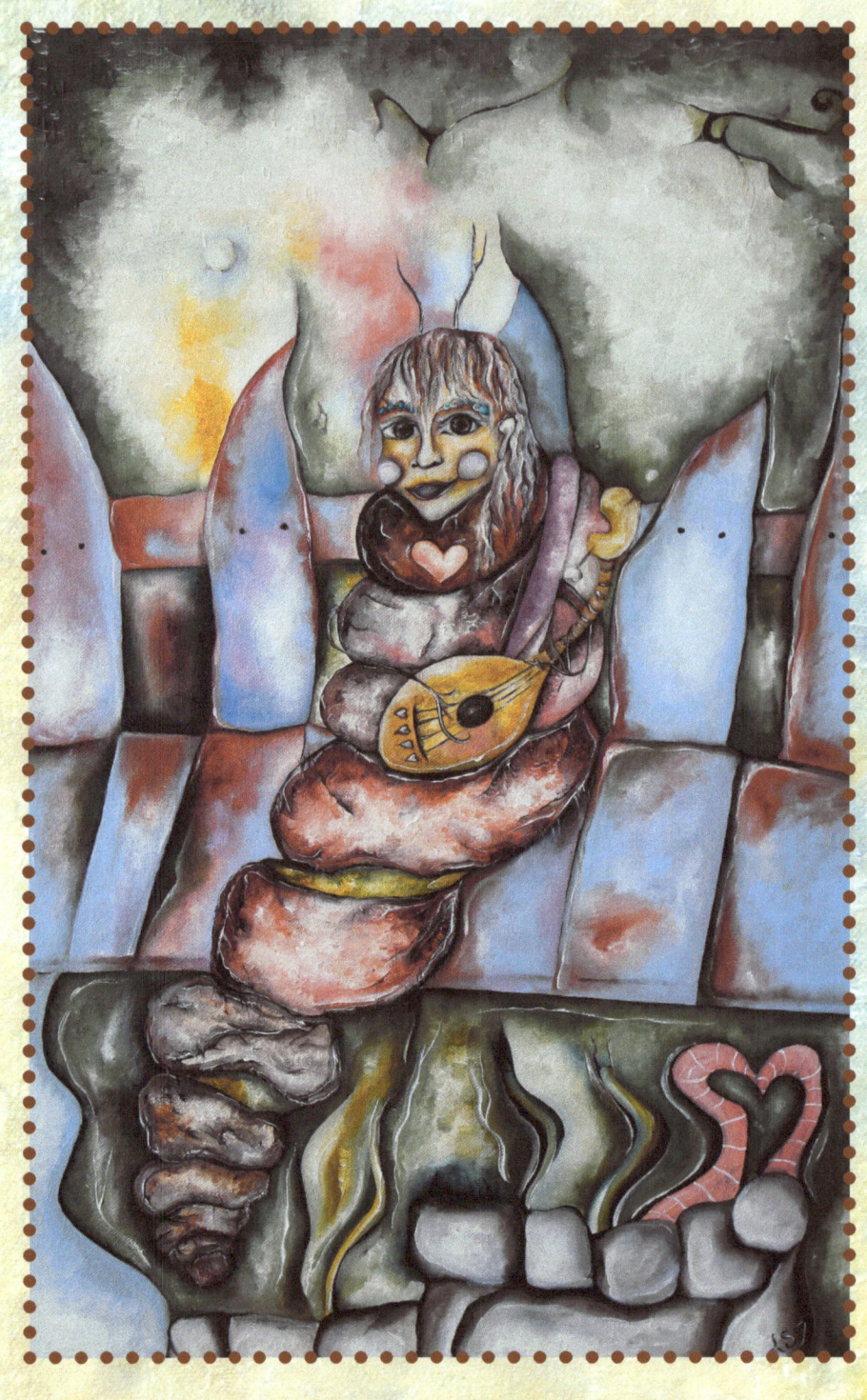

Lily flew back to the limb that rested so sweetly. She laid her head
against her wing and fell back asleep while listening
to Lyssa's song.